Healthcare Fraud?

Let me give you something to think about……

By Angela Renee

Written July 2013

(1)

I constantly hear advertisements and concerns voiced about our country's health care system and the acts of organizations attempting to stop health care related fraud. I am voicing my opinion based on my personal experience. My focus is our healthcare system, in relation to Medicare, specifically the Home Health Care section. I have read where our government has issued procedures that have "cracked down" with the help of organizations such as "HEAP", and that they have been able to recover BILLIONS of dollars with their "crackdown" techniques. I have also read where there have been multiple people made to pay fines in the millions and a lot even doing jail time when investigations on behave of these "crackdown" methods result in a guilty verdict. It makes me wonder "If these crackdowns have resulted in recovering this much money, can you just IMAGINE the amount of money that will never be retrieved?" My thought is that if we are talking this kind of money, if the fraudulent acts didn't occur in the first place, our country's healthcare system probably wouldn't be in trouble it is in now. I also think that some of these "crackdown" procedures are nothing more than the system's organizations attempting to grasp at straws, sort of like trying to grab a few of the straws that are being quickly hauled under water in a raging river. My way of thinking is that if they straws weren't dumped in the raging waters in the first place, there wouldn't be any cause for those feeling the need to grasp a few before they sink. I think more of the focus should be placed on "why" those straws were dumped in the raging waters. If the dumping could be stopped, then that would be the first and foremost step that would prevent our system from sending organizations out to those raging waters and trying their best to grasp a few before sinking down to the bottom.

(2)

Another issue I have is that when those that are sent out with orders to retrieve as many straws as they can, it causes further issues. If those sent out to do the retrieving are offered incentives to grasp as many straws as they can, being human and typically ambitious for incentives, it would be human instinct of survival of the fittest to do whatever needs to be done in order to grasp as many straws as possible. Even if they have to knock others over or to start dragging the bottom of the river in order to collect as many straws as possible to gain incentives. For those who don't appreciate my "metaphorically" way of trying to get my opinion heard, I will speak in a more straight forward way. Again, I want to reiterate that I am only speaking of what I have firsthand experience and knowledge in, which is related to the Home Health Care sector of our Medicare system. Anyone with home health administration experience can tell you that the words "RAC Audit" are words that can send the best of us in a state of mind that wants to run for the hills and take cover. What is a RAC Audit? It's part of our systems organization efforts to send out designated auditors to go through patient records with a fine tooth comb. Their job is to sniff out anything that can be misconstrued or is not TOTALLY in compliance with the (seems like) "trillions" of procedures, COP's (Conditions of Participations), regulations, etc. In my acknowledged experience, if a patient's medical record is not 100% in compliance with every rule, procedure or regulation, then the system has the ability and can/does take back money from the agency and can be given huge fines. It's rare to hear of an agency that has suffered through a RAC Audit and has come out without suffering a detrimental financial experience. Why is this? Are you saying "good, they all deserve it if they couldn't follow all the rules"? If you are saying this, then you must not have the experience in our home health administration world. From my experience, most home health agencies begin with only the very best intentions. The main goal for most of us is being to provide a fabulous service to our senior and disabled population. We want to be this population's advocate and helpmate, doing everything we can to get them as safe, healthy and happy and to be able to stay in their own homes as long as possible. In doing this, and providing this much needed service, we are obligated to provide documentation of every encounter we have with these patients, and all this documentation needs to follow every single rule and regulation that clearly supports the patients need for the service.

(3)

Imagine this scenario (which is a common occurrence) A wonderful nurse (we can call her Mary Ann) with years of experience in home health care that has a passion for helping patients, goes to visit her 6th patient of the day (we can call her Mrs. Patient), Mary Ann makes the day of the widowed Mrs. Patient every week she visits because Mrs. Patient is so lonely. Mary Ann notices that Mrs. Patient legs are extra swollen and she is observed being short of breath. Mary Ann does her assessment on Mrs. Patient and after discussion finds out that Mrs. Patient dropped her prescription of anti-diuretic's (water pills) on the floor 3 days ago and threw them out because she didn't want to swallow any germs. Mary Ann advocates for the Mrs. Patient and calls her doctor. Mary Ann is able to tell the doctor what occurred and what she has observed from her assessment. A new prescription is called in, Mary Ann advocated with Mrs. Patient's son to arrange for pharmacy pick up and to bring the medicine to Mrs. Patient later in the day. Mary Ann instructs Mrs. Patient to call the office if she ever has any further issues with her medicines. Mary Ann continues with her home health visit and changes the dressing on Mrs. Patient's buttock for the pressure ulcer she is being treated for. Mary Ann concludes the home health visit with Mrs. Patient, spending the last minutes of the visit documenting on the nursing visit note. Mary Ann feels good about what she has done for Mrs. Patient today, she feels that if she hadn't gone to see Mrs. Patient, that Mrs Patient would have ended up not being able to breath soon because of her fluid retention issues going on and the fact that she has a history of Congestive Heart Failure (CHF), all of this combined, Mary Ann knows she saved Mrs. Patient from an eventual hospital visit and stay. If you have any idea of what a typical hospital visit and stay costs Medicare, you will know that the service Mary Ann provided on this visit alone has saved Medicare A LOT of money. Instead of a hospital visit, the Mrs. Patient get to get back to "normal" condition in 2 days, takes her medicine as prescribed and get to stay at home, which happens to be the most important thing in her world. Several months go by, Mrs. Patient in no longer receiving home health services because her wound is healed and she no longer has a need for a "skilled service" which is a requirement to receive/provide Medicare home health services. Let's just say that Medicare paid the agency that Mary Ann worked for $1900 for the 60 days of services that Mrs. Patient was eligible for. Several more months go by and the agency Mary Ann works for has visitors at the agency that are there to do a RAC Audit. The auditors are going through Mrs. Patient's medical record. The auditor notices that on a particular visit, the nurse Mary Ann did not clearly indicate that the patient was not home bound, therefore disqualifying her from receiving services and from the agency receiving money. That particular visit was the one we discussed. They determined that as of that visit date, the money should be reimbursed back to Medicare, and because the date of service was only the 3rd visit of the 60-day period that the agency received money for, the reimbursement that Medicare expects back is $1700. Take that away from the $1900 originally paid for the services provided for the 60 day period, and you will get $200 that the agency actually got to keep. Anyone with any home health administration experience will tell you that $200 does not come close to what it cost the agency to provide that service for 60 days. Mary Ann feels terrible because she just plain forgot to document the home bound reasoning on that visit. Did the agency deserve this punishment? This was just a scenario, to get my point across on the "grasping for straws" metaphor that I was talking about. But in reality, these things happen frequently. Does the act of plain human error that occurs to all of us deserve these types of ramifications? This may be a little extreme on my part, but just for intents and purposes, ask yourself this. What would happen if the company you worked for decided to check everyone's handwriting and documentation on correspondence that was business related, whether it by via email, letters, etc...and let's say that they decide that every misspelled word or typo, or any hand written info that they cannot CLEARLY read or interpret from your handwriting, gets you docked $100 for each error because they decide you have shown poor quality of work and incompetence based on their company specifications. What if they found a total of 600 errors on your behave throughout the years you have worked there? How long could you survive?

(4)

Again, I will go back to why I began these examples to begin with. Grasping at straws to attempt to save our healthcare system and stop fraudulent activity will not have the long term effect that is needed. For every technique our government's organizations will come up with to attempt to hold accountable for those doing fraudulent activities, there will most likely by 10 times more of the individuals/organizations that will always come up with other ways. If someone wants to become a known fraudulent felon and intentionally sets out to perform fraudulent acts in order to gain success out of our Medicare system, I do hope they are stopped sooner rather than later. I believe there will always be those with criminal mind sets just as well as there will always be common humor errors. I wish our government organizations would focus stronger on stopping it from happening in the beginning, than using techniques that punish normal operating agencies on common human error.

(5)

I want to share my thoughts that will hopefully shed some light on an avenue that our government organizations CAN control and make a difference from the very beginning (to stop the straws from being dumped into the raging waters to begin with)....Let's say we have a criminal minded person who has researched to ways to get rich schemes by using fraudulent means to get a couple million dollars from Medicare. We will make this person a male, and we will name him Joe Shmo. Joe Shmo's mom had a recent surgery and needed home health care when she came home. His mom needed Physical Therapy, Occupational Therapy, a Nurse and a Home Health Aide for several weeks. His mom did real good and made a complete recovery. A few weeks after she stopped receiving home health services, Joe Shmo was over her house for dinner. Joe Shmo seen some open mail on the table and started to read it. It was a Medicare claim notice that stated that the home health agency that provided his moms services were given $5500. Joe Shmo thinks "wow" I am in the wrong business. I could be rich in no time if I was getting that kind of money. As Joe Shmo has always had criminally minded schemes going on, he begins to think of ways to get into this wonderfully paying system. He wants to make a million ASAP, and move to Costa Rica where he will live like a king for the rest of his life. Joe Shmo sets out trying to figure out how to go about this. He gets really excited when he discovers everything he needs to know with a few clinks on the internet. He researches plenty of fraudulent Medicare activity related to home health care and thinks the people that got caught where never as smart as he is, and that they just got too greedy. All he wants is to make a quick million ASAP, change names and head out of the country. He finds everything he needs to know about how to start a home health agency that can bill Medicare within the hour on the internet. He is feeling lucky because he already lives in a state that does not require any special licensing to even get started. He figures that he could be up and running, ready to start sending Medicare a bunch of fraudulent bills within the next several months. All he has to do is follow the few simple steps to get the ball rolling. He gets on the internet and finds a company that will do everything for him for a $299 fee to get a legal name for the business, he could even have his business be real legit with being an LLC. He decides to name his home health agency Shmo's BEST Home Care. He doesn't want to have to use his name if he can help it, but he realizes that he is going to have to open a bank account with the agencies name because he will have to prove he has a legit business and show he has $30K in the bank ready and waiting to be available for business purposes….After thinking, he comes up with a great solution. He will use his dad's name, which happens to be Joe Shmo also, and he thinks "man this is really gonna work out easy cause dad put my name on his savings account years ago, so I can just have the name on that account changed to Shmo's BEST Home Care. He doesn't plan on stealing from his dad's account because is way too low life. He figures no harm done, all he needs it for is to prove the business has an account with the name of the business and showing it has at least $30K in it for business use. No problem Joe Shmo thinks. This is gonna be too easy..Costa Rica, here I come baby!!!! Joe Shmo puts all his efforts into this wonderful business idea, researching and making sure he has everything he had read in place and ready to go. He discovered a few obstacles that took some time to think through, but he was a smart man and could do anything he put his mind to, he was determined. One obstacle was figuring he needed to set up a small office somewhere to make it look like he had a real business going. He took out some money from the account, but figured he would put that back in no time and Dad would never even know. His cousin Richy Shmo had a shop in the neighborhood and knew Richy would let him use that one little room in the back to clean up and make his business office. Richy also had a girlfriend named Stelly that was a home health aide and wore scrubs to work. Richy and Stelly were always looking to make a quick buck, so Joe Shmo figured he would cut Richy and Stelly in on the deal. He told them his plans and they were all for it. Richy figured once Joe Shmo skipped town with money in the bank, he would just say he didn't know the guy; he just rented him some space. Stelly was excited about making a bundle herself and didn't have any problem using the name of a person named Nella Nohow. Joe Shmo explained that he needed Stelly to pretend to be Nella Nohow, a nurse that lived in the same town that he found when he was looking at the nurse's registry on the internet. Joe Shmo needed Stelly to pretend to be this nurse for when the person from a government agency came to do a survey. He explained he would make her a badge, have a personnel file on her and everything. Stella was excited to play actress, she always wanted to be a nurse. No problem. They also added Stelly's little sister Wella, in on the game. Wella's job at the time of the survey was going to become Stelly so she could use her name and ID and prove she was a home health aide. Those were the only people Joe Shmo needed to involve. He researched that he could show he was operating a home health agency with only providing a nurse and a home health aide. That problem solved. Another obstacle that took some thought was getting some patients together to get through this survey process. He read that the surveyor will actually go out to visit some of these patients along with either Stelly or Wella while they pretended to do their jobs. He knew all about the "home bound" thing from his research, knew what all had to be documented on the fake visit notes and everything. This obstacle turned out too easy also, he had many friends and cousins in the neighborhood with grandparents and aunts and uncles. It was pretty easy to find people he could trust to play along in case the surveyor wanted to visit them. Every one of them was happy to make the promised $500 if they played their part right as a patient that was receiving services. Joe Shmo explained to them that he was getting this business together to give to his cousin Richy and Stelly for a wedding gift so that they could have a business to make money on for their 3 kids. No one had a problem playing along, not when they would be helping out the neighborhood folks and friends, and making $500 in the process. That amount was unheard of in this neighborhood. Joe Shmo got online an ordered some forms he needed and a policy and procedure manual that he would need to show. Everything was in place and ready. The last obstacle was getting this survey thing done, that was going to be the toughest obstacle to overcome and he was actually getting a little nervous and being face to face with some surveyor that would make or break his new business. But he knew he could do it, he was smart and did all the research on what to expect...He was ready for them.... Joe Shmo ended up taking a bit more money out of the account to pay for the forms, a desk, file cabinet, the manual and a couple other things that the found he needed to have organized in binders and stuff. He was really glad he could access the account because he had to end up paying for this survey too. It was a couple grand, but no problem, he would put all that with some extra in just a couple months. His plan was coming along real nice, but he admitted to himself he actually had to work at this thing pretty hard to make it all look legit. He was ready for this. Joe Shmo even had 60 older people he knew of in the neighborhood that he was prepared to bill Medicare for as soon as he got through this survey and was able to start sending bills to Medicare. It was easy to find the first 60 people's information. He broke into the local clinic's office one night and went through some patient files to get the information he needed to send Medicare some bills. He was only there for an hour and got 60 already. He figured he would go back in a couple weeks and get more patient information; it was easy the first time. He wanted to get the money from Medicare in his account ASAP and get out of town with his ill-gotten gains. He figured it would take weeks after he got paid for everything for anyone to even find out. His mom didn't get her notice in the mail for several weeks afterwards. He would be long gone before all those people even got the mail. So now, all he had left to do was wait for this survey, which should be at any time now. His plan was to send a message to Stelly and Wella on the day the surveyor got there to the office, so that they could dress in scrubs and put on their name badges and get into the office to make it look like they were real workers. He didn't really like having to get up every morning during the week and he got lazy about getting to the "office" by 9:00am every morning, where he hung out to see if the surveyor would finally show up. Joe Shmo knew from what he read that the accrediting organization that was coming out to do his survey wouldn't be giving him any notice because he wanted to be able to bill Medicare, this survey had to be "unannounced" (we will talk more in detail about this issue later on), so he tried really hard to be at the office space every morning, but some mornings he just didn't want to crawl out of bed. The accrediting organization that he signed up for and paid to come out to do his survey had a special website for "providers" which is proudly was. On that website there was a message place you could click on that said "unannounced surveys will be posted here at 7:30am local time on the day of the survey" Joe Shmo thought to himself, no way man, no way could that be real, cause my research said it was from some federal procedure thing that said his type of survey called "deemed status" HAD to be "unannounced"…so Jo Shmo just figured that this website thing was wrong, but just in case, he set his alarm for 7:30 am every morning just to check to see if the accrediting organization would be kind enough to actually let him know they were coming out. That would be too great thinks Joe Shmo, not gonna happen….One particular morning Joe Shmo was still in bed at 7:30 am with a headache, he figured he was just gonna sleep in and forget about the office thing cause he needed to catch up on some sleep from a late night. When the alarm went off at 7:30 am, he half opened his eyes just to log onto the internet site just in case. His eyes popped wide open when he seen that he was scheduled for his survey that day, it had the picture and name of the surveyor too. This was Joe Shmo's lucky day by far. He wouldn't have been able to get his survey if he hadn't known they were coming because he planned on just sleeping through this day. Joe Shmo thinks "this must be fate man". So as Shmo's BEST Home Care didn't open its office until 9:00 am, Jo Shmo knew he had time to get everything in place at the last moment. He went ahead and called

Stelly and Wella and told them to look alive, it was game day. The plan was for Stelly to call a few "patients" too and let me know to look alive that today was the day. Jo Shmo was nervous and excited; the final step to his life time in Costa Rica was finally here. The surveyor showed up about 9:15 am. Jo Shmo, Stelly and Wella were ready and waiting, sitting around the office pretending like they knew what they were doing. Jo Shmo introduced himself and owner and operator, with his made up personnel file showing he had tons of experience in health care management, ready and waiting. He introduces Stelly and Wella as the well-rehearsed fakes they were pretending to be. It was "GAME ON"...... Joe Shmo answered some questions from the surveyor and then just started giving her what she asked for, either it be the manuals, employee records, patient records, whatever... everything was going smooth Joe Shmo thought. He bought lunch every day for the surveyor just to get on her good side and pretended to be the upstanding citizen he was not. The surveyor ended up staying for 2 days to get everything she needed. When she was just about done, she handed Joe Shmo a list of "problems" she had found with patient records. She stated to Joe Shmo "Things don't look very good here". Joe Shmo wanted to know why, he researched that even if the surveyor found "problems" that he would be able to do some kind of plans of actions to fix things, then everything would be fine, he figured it just might take a few extra weeks if that happened. When the surveyor pointed to the notes she wrote down on a piece of paper for Joe Shmo, and said "from all the patient safety issues I found that I wrote down for you, it will most likely be that you will have to go through another survey in order to prove you are operating sufficiently, there is just too much wrong with what I am seeing that cannot be corrected with a plan of action"....Joe Shmo felt like he just lost his best friend, he seen his life ambitions going down the tubes, all his hard work for nothing. He decided to be the smart person he was and decided at a moment's notice to play at gaining some sympathy to see if he could change her mind. After all, she hadn't actually put anything on her report just yet, she just handed him some hand written paper notes with her findings. Joe Shmo laid it on thick. He pretended to be a sad little boy, told the surveyor he was sorry, but that he was trying so hard to make a difference for people that he sometimes forgot to follow the rules. He continued with a sob story about how his mother had passed away just months ago, and that it took a toll on him. Joe Shmo was ecstatic when he realized he had gotten to the surveyor with his made up drama. He thought he had died and gone to Heaven when she hugged him and said, I understand, and that's why I like to give you the things I find in writing before I put them in a report. Let's look at these things together and see what we can do. The surveyor told Joe Shmo that she was not going to report everything she found, that she was going to leave out the "really bad things" that couldn't be corrected with a plan of action. She received a requested promise from Joe Shmo to "make sure these things are fixed".... Over the next several weeks Joe Shmo received his report from the accrediting organization and sure enough, all he had to do was send back some plans of actions to fix the few things the surveyor ended up reporting. Within a few more months, Joe Shmo finally received his Medicare Billing Number....Life was good for

Joe Shmo. To place an ending on my fictional story involving Joe Shmo, he ended up in Costa Rica 4 months later living under another name, and living the lifestyle of a celebrity.

(6)

Now, I will go back to the reason why I invented the Joe Shmo story for you. I wanted people to be able to put into perspective my reasoning and thinking that our governmental organizations need to focus on fixing things from the beginning before they can expect to see a positive outcome from stopping fraudulent activity. Had the accrediting organization that came out to do the "deemed status" survey for Shmo's BEST Home Care had NOT gone against the rules set in place and announced that they were coming, Joe Shmo wouldn't have had the survey to begin with and wouldn't have taken off with millions more of our Medicare money. The reason WHY the regulations are in place that state clearly that an agency seeking "deemed status" MUST have the survey "UNANNOUNCED"…… In Joe Shmo's case, if the office was not operating as required and no one appeared "home" at the time of the survey that would have been the first "red flag" that the agency was not operating sufficiently, the survey would NOT have taken place and Joe Shmo would have had to restart his process. Why would an accrediting organization go against their own rules and the rules of the government organization and actually announce an unannounced survey visit? This is my thought, the accrediting organization got tired of losing money when they would show up for surveys and not find anyone at home. All they get to keep at that point would be the non-refundable deposit made, but would lose out on the several more thousands that they could earn by the survey actually getting done.

Another lesson to take to the heart of the matter is the surveyor's procedures of collecting information. In the Joe Shmo story, it puts a real imagine on what actually happens out in the real world. I have heard and read so many different people complaining of surveyor's ethics and interchangeable procedures based on their own preference. Why is it that some hospitals, home care agencies or other health care facility have a survey done and come out with gold metals and smelling like roses, when others have a survey done and come out of it in a near bankrupt state because of the fines and such? I believe that the main difference between a hospital having a survey smelling like roses and the hospital having to suffer major consequences is mainly due to the surveyors. I believe ALL surveys should be conducted the SAME way at ALL times by EVERY surveyor. Our governing officials place these accrediting organizations in a very high place in our health care world. The surveyors and accrediting organizations that we health care providers are forced to use to do business, need to take off the crowns they wear. THEY need to be held responsible for fair treatment of all. THEY should not be permitted to show favoritism when they have the urge to. THEY should not be growing nice bank accounts operating under their own rules while getting to wear the immunity crown that our government grants them. Our governmental associates need to take the power back. Take it out of the hands of these accrediting organizations that are abusive with the power they are given.

Instead of keeping the grant of "immunity" alive for these accrediting organizations, they need to be held accountable at even higher standard than us health care providers out here trying to do everything we can to make an actual difference for our people.

(7)

Our country's healthcare system is in the gutter as everyone knows. Everyone wants to encourage someone else to "blow the whistle"…..leaving too much room for false allegations that damage innocent people/organizations. Our people are only human, and as humans they will take advantage of most any opportunity to fulfill a selfish need (usually relating to money). If the government wants to seriously make needed changes, they need to start at the top. As my metaphorically speaking story towards the beginning implies... WE WILL HAVE BETTER OUTCOMES WITH SERIOUS CHANGES NEEDED IF WE STOP THE STRAWS FROM GETTING DUMPED IN THE RAGING WATERS....

I have used a lot of metaphorically and fictional story telling in order to paint my picture. I operate a home health care business. I am accredited and certified. I will tell you truthfully without metaphors that the accrediting sorganizations that I utilized mislead me and falsified information from the beginning with me. The organization announced just as explained in my Joe Shmo story that they were coming to do my "deemed status" survey. My surveyor provided me notes similar to the notes I wrote about in the Joe Shmo story, which she kindly did not include in the report. WHY? Because she had the power to........

(Ending Comments)

My hope in writing this is that someone, somewhere can pay real attention to the complaints and concerns that health care providers have been voicing for years about the accrediting organizations that have been granted immunity for wrong doings, and still continue to wear the crowns placed upon them by our government.

If anyone is interested in starting their own home health agency, please get with me. Let me share my personal experience to that you can hopefully avoid my mistakes.

Best wishes everyone, we are all going to need them ☺

Angela Renee

www.ingramcontent.com/pod-product-compliance
Lightning Source LLC
Chambersburg PA
CBHW071551170526
45166CB00004B/1632